HOW THEY LIVED

A COLONIAL AMERICAN MERCHANT

ROBIN MAY

Illustrated by Mark Bergin

ROURKE ENTERPRISES, INC.
Vero Beach, Florida 32964

First published in the
United States in 1987 by
Rourke Enterprises, Inc.
PO Box 3328, Vero Beach,
Florida 32964

First Published in 1986 by
Wayland (Publishers) Limited
61 Western Road, Hove
East Sussex BN3 1JD, England

© Copyright 1986 Wayland (Publishers) Limited

Typeset by Kalligraphics Ltd, Redhill, Surrey
Printed in Italy by G. Canale & C.S.p.A., Turin

Library of Congress Cataloging-in-Publication Data

May, Robin.
A colonial American merchant.

(How they lived)
Bibliography: p.
Includes index.
Summary: Describes the life of a Colonial
merchant, his business, family life, home, social
life, and his role in the War of Independence.
Includes a glossary of terms.
1. United States – Social life and customs –
Colonial period, ca. 1600–1775 – Juvenile literature.
2. Merchants – United States – History – Juvenile literature.
[1. United States – Social life and customs –
Colonial period, ca. 1600–1775. 2. Merchants
I. Bergin, Mark ill. II. Title. III. Series:
How they lived (Vero Beach, Fla.)
E162.M34   1987   973.2   86–20261
ISBN 0–86592–139–3

CONTENTS

THE SHIP COMES IN

The harbor was like a forest of sails and masts, and the merchant never grew tired of the sight. He had come to America with nothing. Now he owned a small fleet of trading ships. Yesterday one had arrived with sugar from the West Indies. In a few days another ship would bring manufactured goods from England.

The port was Boston nearly 300 years ago. It was the largest city in English-speaking North America and had prospered because of fishing, trading and whaling. Only London and Bristol had more ships in the English-speaking world. Down the coast from Boston were other great city-ports where wealthy merchants lived. America was a land of opportunity, not just for the wealthy, but for all the colonists.

The Spanish and French had settled in North America before the English came. The first successful

English colony was founded at Jamestown, Virginia, in 1607. People came there in search of gold, and it soon grew into a trading center. In 1620 the famous Pilgrim Fathers started a settlement at Plymouth, which later became the colony of Massachusetts. They had sailed from England to find religious freedom. From these beginnings would one day come the United States of America.

THE THIRTEEN COLONIES

Between 1607 and 1733, thirteen English colonies were founded in what is now the United States of America. They stretched along the Atlantic coast from New Hampshire in the north to Georgia in the south.

People came from the "Old World" to the "New World" in search of a new, better life for themselves and their families.

Many also wished to worship God in the particular way that they wanted. The people who crossed the Atlantic in those early years were mostly English, but Scots, Irish, Welsh, Germans, Dutch and Swedes came as well. The French settled to the north in Canada, while the Spanish came to the south and west.

The English depended on trade with England. In the north, colonists lived on the coast or on inland farms and in villages. The farms were small, as the ground was rocky and

the climate fairly cool. Fortunately the waters teemed with fish, as the colonists of Massachusetts, New Hampshire, Connecticut and Rhode Island soon discovered.

Farther south in New York, New Jersey, Delaware, Pennsylvania and Maryland, the weather was warmer and farms were bigger. The southern colonies of Virginia, North and South Carolina and Georgia, were warmer and produced tobacco, cotton and rice.

Some colonies were ruled by the King of England; others by a "proprietor" who was paid by the King. Others were "corporate" colonies with a charter from the King.

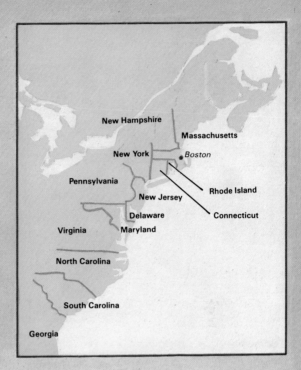

The thirteen English colonies in 1700.

Arriving in the New World was an exciting prospect for the early settlers.

COLONIAL TOWNS

Although the farm was the center of many colonists' lives, villages sprang up everywhere and many became towns. A town had a church and its own local government. If it was near a river and had one or more roads running through it, a town would grow much faster.

The towns that grew fastest were those with good harbors. Trade and manufacturing depended on five towns in particular – New York, Boston, Charleston, Newport, and Philadelphia, which was the largest manufacturing center.

These and other towns were often most impressive. In 1720 an English traveler, seeing Boston, said: "A gentleman from London would almost think himself at home."

Early colonial towns had many fine buildings.

Another saw over 3,000 houses, a third of them built of brick.

Brick was widely used but wood was plentiful and much cheaper for ordinary people. Therefore wooden frame houses were popular. There were also splendid mansions like those in England. The famous "log cabin" was introduced in the 1600s by Swedish settlers, who copied the cabins of their homeland. In the warm South, rich citizens of Charleston built houses one room wide but up to four storys high. This was so that sea breezes would keep them cool.

A view of New York's waterfront in the eighteenth century.

A MERCHANT'S HOUSE

The 18th century was a period of beautiful houses for those who could afford them. A successful colonial merchant could live in as fine a house as he wanted to, and furnish it as well as any English merchant across the Atlantic. No visiting Englishman who was prosperous would feel out of place in an American mansion, many of which were built in the Georgian style (architecture of the period between 1715 and 1820).

Many merchants' houses were square buildings with high windows and a fine front door. They were

Wealthy merchants lived in impressive town houses.

often built of red brick. Inside, a large hall and sweeping staircase led to a number of wood-paneled rooms. There was no space for a big garden. These were very much town houses.

A merchant's furniture was very handsome. At this time there were great furniture makers in England, and American ones also became expert. Tables that could be folded to make them smaller were popular, as were big four-poster beds. A

Merchant homes were comfortable and elegantly furnished.

merchant would sleep on a feather mattress and could pull curtains around the bed on cold nights.

One piece of furniture was the invention of the scientist and statesman, Benjamin Franklin. It was the rocking chair, and it soon became very popular throughout Amercia.

11

WORKING LIFE

A successful merchant usually had to get up early, for he had so much to do. He might start out with a single ship, then build up a fleet of his own.

Some merchants had been ships' captains while others owned shipyards. One merchant, Philip English, started out as captain of a small ship in about 1670; by 1692 he owned twenty-one. He had his own wharf at Salem, Massachusetts, and thirteen buildings. He also had a grand mansion in the town. A successful merchant was welcome in London, in Europe and in every great house in his town.

A merchant's headquarters at the docks was an exciting place, but also a worrisome one. Without today's communications, he could not know when his ships would arrive. A ship might sail into the harbor six weeks late, having been blown far off course by high winds. There was always a possibility that his ships might be attacked by pirates.

Merchants were meant to trade only with England – so Parliament had ordered. However, orders were easy to disobey. Since most merchants regarded themselves as freeborn Englishmen, they were prepared to trade with any nation. No wonder some made huge fortunes!

Left *Merchant ships spent weeks at sea, as they sailed to distant countries.*

Right *A merchant often discussed weather and trading conditions with his ship's captain.*

FAMILY LIFE

A butler receiving visitors into a merchant's home.

A rich merchant in the American colonies was definitely a member of America's upper class. Family life for him was very different from that of ordinary folk. Yet it was far easier in America than it was in England for people to lift themselves from poverty to riches and real importance in a community. Only slaves had no hope of improvement, except for a kind master or, perhaps, freedom.

A merchant worked as hard as any of his workers and sailors. However, his home life was much more comfortable than theirs. He could enjoy the best food and drink and entertain his friends in grand style. He might have a black slave who acted as his butler and, perhaps, a black or white cook. His children might have a black nurse to look after them.

The colony's Governor probably dined with merchant families from time to time. Sons of merchants might study law in England, or follow their father's footsteps in the family business. A merchant's daughter was very likely to marry the son of another leading family.

In early times, conversation in a merchant's house in a northern colony might well be about religion. By the 1700s, families would be talking

A portrait by John Hesselius showing the boy Charles Calvert with a servant (1761).

more and more about politics and the rights of colonies to have a say in their own government. Dinner parties in the home of a colonial merchant must have been very lively!

SLAVES AND SERVANTS

We have seen that colonial Americans were not as divided into classes as their relations back in Britain. People could move up to the upper class if they did well. But there was one class of people who could never move up in society.

These were the black slaves. They were brought from Africa to America and the West Indies by the thousands. They were also taken to colonies owned by European nations in Central and South America.

In England's southern colonies in America, slaves mainly worked on cotton, rice and tobacco plantations, without pay and without hope. Even those who worked in their master's house had no rights. Slaves could be beaten to death, and their families split up. Only a few were allowed to go free.

Northern slaves worked in homes, factories and in the docks. In general,

Harvesting tobacco was hot, exhausting work.

their lives were not so terrible. Slavery gradually died out in the North, but did not vanish from the South until 1865. That was after the American Civil War had been fought, mainly over the question of slavery.

There were also "indentured" servants in colonial times, who came to America to serve a master for between four and seven years. "Indentured" meant that they had signed a contract. The servant's journey to America was paid and he or she was looked after, but not paid until the years had been served. Then the person was free to make his own way in the world.

Only the wealthy could afford to smoke tobacco.

SCHOOLS

The children of rich colonists were often taught in their own homes by private teachers, called tutors. Others went to private schools. In New England, Latin Grammar schools were started in towns of a certain size. A merchant's children might go to one of them if he could afford the fees. If he was very rich he would probably hire a tutor.

Churches ran schools, too. Basic education was given at the Latin Grammer schools, as well as some Greek and Latin. After leaving school, a bright pupil might go to a college. The first one to be opened

A private lesson with a tutor.

was in Harvard, Massachusetts, which dates from 1636. Some colonies had laws that made towns open schools for all. These were paid for by taxes.

A Quaker merchant in Pennsylvania would send his children to schools where not only Latin and Greek were taught, but also mathematics. The children were also taught some useful trade or skill.

A merchant's children might start at a "dame" school, run by a woman in her home. They learned spelling, writing and arithmetic. Poorer children often learned a trade from a craftsman, who had apprentices and gave them some education. A merchant would later be able to use their skills. He might have been an apprentice himself.

This old engraving shows children in a Delaware school.

COLONIAL FASHIONS

A successful merchant in colonial America wore the latest European style of clothes. Rich plantation owners would do the same, along with other prosperous people and their families. They were just as smart as fashionable Londoners.

Their clothes might be made in England or, more probably, the materials for them would be sent across the Atlantic. They would then be made up by an expert local tailor.

In colonial America, long wigs were fashionable. These might be covered with white powder. For a time, late in the colonial period, ladies' wigs soared higher and higher, supported by a frame. Men's wigs gradually became simpler and began to look more like ordinary hair.

Naturally, most people wore far simpler clothes. Children did not have their own fashions, but were dressed like miniature adults. Ordinary people made their own clothes. The fleece of sheep was spun into yarn to provide woolen clothes. Linen was woven from flax. Shoes and leggings were handmade from

Some ladies were very skilled at sewing and spinning.

Left *The latest European fashions were popular among prosperous colonists.*

skins, and shoemaking was a profitable trade. The clothes of ordinary folk might be rough and simple, but these homemade garments served their wearers well.

21

RELIGION

A colonial merchant, like nearly all Americans of his time, was almost certainly a churchgoer. Rich and poor would worship together. This did not mean that they were all considered equal, except in the eyes of God. Upper class people, such as merchants, sat in better pews.

As a leading citizen, a merchant would also appear in church at meetings to discuss town business. He would no doubt talk with other merchants after a service.

If the merchant was a Puritan of New England, he would be convinced that he and the other Puritans were the only people who were worshiping God in the right way. They did not allow the friendly Quakers to be citizens of New England. Meanwhile, a Southern merchant was probably a member of the

Going to church was an important event for the colonists.

Anglican Church, that is, the Church of England.

Even a powerful merchant could not avoid trouble in New England if he argued with his church's leaders. This was especially so in the early days. One important merchant's wife, Mrs. Anne Hutchinson, dared to disagree with some of the harsh ideas the Puritans taught. She was hauled into court and banished. At least she was not hanged as a witch, like some. Happily for many, the Puritans lost some of their power in later years.

The Pilgrim Fathers landed in the New World in 1620. They came to seek religious freedom.

FOOD AND DRINK

Most colonial Americans enjoyed better food than their relations back in England. There was plenty of wildlife to hunt and seafood to catch, and much of the land was good for farming. Merchants and their families could expect to eat very well.

A wealthy merchant would give dinner parties and invite other leading citizens. He would provide good wines and his servants or slaves would wait on the table. The silverware was very fine, as were the tablecloths. Like the dishes from which the food was served, they had probably come from England.

A merchant could afford beef, but ordinary people were more likely to eat pork. There was fish in abundance. In the winter, smoked or salted meat would be eaten, plus vegetables that were stored in a celler.

Merchants enjoyed tea and chocolate to drink, and coffee began to be more and more popular. A merchant, unlike most people, could afford sugar and spices.

Early merchants and their families used a knife and their fingers at meals, but later on forks were used instead of fingers.

Below *A Puritan family say grace before a meal.*

Right *Rich merchants enjoyed holding lavish dinner parties.*

GAMES AND PASTIMES

Many merchants were too busy to have much time for leisure activities. How much entertainment a merchant's family could enjoy depended on where they lived. A merchant living in South Carolina could enjoy the theater. Actors were always welcome there and in other colonies, but they were not well received in New England.

In 1867, a Puritan named Increase Mather heard that plays were coming to his area. He and other solemn Puritans saw to it that actors were not allowed to visit for another hundred years. Puritans and

Many people enjoyed theater trips, although some Puritans disapproved.

Horseracing was a popular pastime.

Quakers both thought that the theater was the "devil's schoolhouse"!

Southerners could enjoy music, but it took years for New Englanders to be allowed to hear anything but church music in public. Fortunately, there were books and newspapers to read, though some Puritans objected to newspapers as they were entertaining!

Horseracing, including trotting races, was widely enjoyed. A merchant could own a race horse and enjoy hunting. Dancing was especially popular with Virginian planters and merchants alike, and dancing masters and musicians were welcome all over the South. Despite the anger of Puritans, there was even some dancing in the New England colonies. Fortunately, merchants could relax in coffee houses and clubs without being rebuked by the serious Puritans.

HEALTH

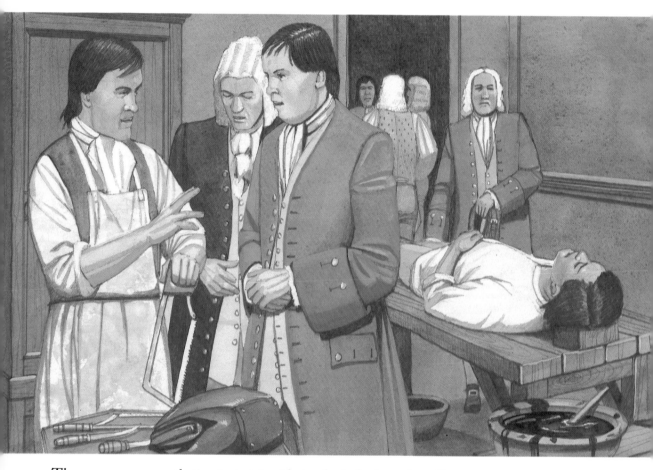

There were no anesthetics to put people to sleep during operations.

Like the rest of the world in the 1600s and 1700s, the American colonists could not expect much help from doctors. Illness could strike rich merchants and poor workers alike. Both needed luck to survive illness and both had to endure surgery without being put to sleep first.

Poorer people and the Indians knew of herbs that helped cure or relieve illnesses. Some merchants had scientific friends who were trying to improve medical knowledge. These scientists studied herbal cures and other possible remedies. Killer diseases, like smallpox, diphtheria, and cholera killed merchants and workers alike. Unfortunately, few people knew that dirty conditions encouraged outbreaks of disease.

A merchant who became ill would be looked after at home, not in a public hospital. Merchants had a particular interest in the disease called scurvy that weakened or killed their sailors. It was caused by lack of vitamin C, and could be avoided by eating oranges, lemons and limes. However, this was not widely known until after the colonial period.

Fortunately, most colonists enjoyed better food and healthier living conditions than their relations in Europe, so their health was generally better.

People would lie in bed for weeks if they became ill.

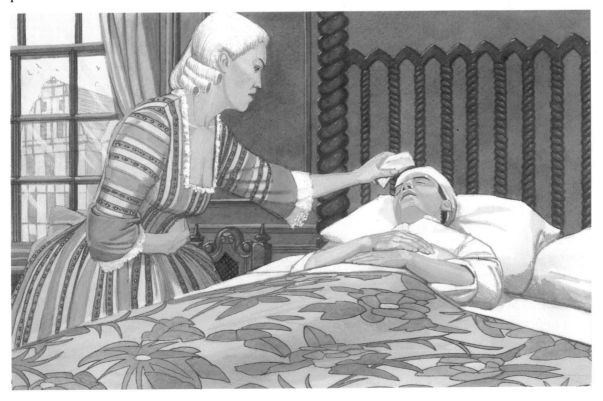

THE COLONIES BREAK AWAY

In 1759 Britain and America celebrated the capture of Quebec, the capital of French Canada, by English troops. The colonists were thus free from the threat of a French invasion. In 1760 they toasted their new king, George III. Yet in 1775 war broke out between the colonies and the Mother Country, England. What had gone wrong?

We have seen how independent the colonists were in their refusal to trade only with Britain. Now, with no Americans in Parliament, they protested: "No taxation without representation!" Were they not British, too? In 1776 the colonies declared themselves free from British rule. The War of Independence ended in 1783. The United States of America was born.

As for the merchants, many had prospered from the war. They turned their ships into privateers – government-backed pirate ships – and many made huge fortunes.

The Boston Tea Party (December 16, 1773) was a protest against taxation.

GLOSSARY

American Civil War (1861–65) The war between the United States government and eleven of the southern states.

American War of Independence (1775–83) The war between the settlers of the thirteen English colonies in America and their homeland. The colonists wanted to become independent from English rule.

Colony A community formed by people who settle in a country far away from their homeland.

England Nearly all the original American colonists were from England, not the rest of Britain.

French Canada England and her American colonies were often at war with France, which owned Canada until 1760.

Indians The original inhabitants of North America.

New World When America was first discovered, it was thought of as a "new" world.

Plantation A large farm where crops are grown.

Puritans These people were sober-living Protestants who wanted to purify the Church of England from Catholicism.

Quakers Members of a religious group called the Society of Friends.

INDEX

Picture acknowledgments

The pictures in this book were supplied by the following: By Courtesy of the Baltimore Museum of Art 15; Mary Evans Picture Library 9, 17; The Mansell Collection 12, 30; Peter Newark's Western Americana 19, 23 (inset), 24; By Courtesy of The Victoria and Albert Museum 21.